过年了!

请给我糖果!

请给我饺子!

请给我年糕!

请给我新衣服!

请给我放鞭炮!

请给我红包!

请给我拜年!

Glossary

	Pinyin	English Definition
过年	guò nián	to celebrate the Chinese New Year
请	qǐng	please
给	gěi	to give
糖果	táng guǒ	candy
饺子	jiǎo zi	dumpling
年糕	nián gāo	rice cake
新	xīn	new
衣服	yī fu	clothing
放鞭炮	fàng biān pào	to set off firecrackers
红包	hóng bāo	money wrapped in red envelopes as a gift
拜年	bài nián	to pay a New Year call

Copyright © 2022 by Level Learning INC.

All rights reserved. No part of this book in whole or part may be reproduced without written permission from the publisher

Author: Jingyao Qi, Level Learning

Simplified Chinese Edition

- This is the last page of this book. -

www.ingramcontent.com/pod-product-compliance
Lightning Source LLC
Chambersburg PA
CBHW042225090526
44583CB00001BA/24